How to Avoid Probate

and manage your assets from the grave

Jim Clark

Published by

J. Charles Clark Publishing
a division of J. Charles Clark Consulting, Inc.
a member of the Clark Group of American Companies

ISBN 978-0-578-18015-1

Printed in the United States of America

Revised 2021

Special Dedication

This book is dedicated to my little Michelle Maria, who liked to go for ice cream with her daddy. She read the menu upside down every time, until she made the same decision every time, cherry pie and coke. Then, one day she stopped reading the menu and started reading the law. Now she is a fine attorney, cherry pie and coke, right side up. My little Michelle Maria.

Foreword

This book needed to be written, and I'm glad my friend Jim Clark wrote it.

Jim Clark and I have collaborated on estate planning cases for well over 25 years. He has a brilliant mind, and a special talent for making complicated matters easy to understand; he has certainly hit the mark this time.

After practicing law as an estate-planning attorney for over 58 years, I can attest that the legal concepts discussed are accurate.

The book is just plain fun to read; I give it a thumbs up. Well done, Jim.

Robert C. Ware, AB, J.D.
Attorney at Law

Table of Contents

The smart way to transfer your assets to your heirs is to use a document know as a Revocable Living Trust.

Wills | Probate

There are two ways to do anything. There's the easy way, and the hard way; the smart way, and the not-so-smart way. Generally, the smart way is the less expensive way. And, so it is with transferring your assets to your heirs when you die.

The smart way to transfer your assets to your heirs is to use a document known as a Revocable Living Trust; the not-so-smart way is to use a document known as a Will. The reason is simple. Any assets you transfer to your heirs using a will are considered part of your probate estate; they are considered to have "gone through probate" Putting your assets through probate is a problem; in fact, it's three problems.

First, the probate process is public. Your will, will be recorded at the courthouse, which means anyone who wants to know what you left to your heirs, or to whom you left it, can easily find out; they have only to visit the courthouse and read your will. Should they desire to do so, they can have a copy made and mail it to 300 of their closest friends.

Second, probate is expensive. Depending upon the size of your estate, probate expenses can range in the tens of thousands of dollars or more. That can be a lot of money to waste, especially when you don't have to. When was the last time you took a $100.00 bill out of your pocket and set fire to it just for the fun of watching it burn, ever?

Third, probate can be very hard on your family. Many families have been torn apart going through the probate process. In 399 B.C., Socrates said: "A son can suffer the loss of his parents with great equanimity, but the loss of his estate drives him to despair." I know Socrates said this because he told me in person one afternoon while we were helping Hypocrites write the Hippocratic Oath.

Socrates said: “A son can suffer the loss of his parents with great equanimity, but the loss of his estate drives him to despair”.

Wills | Probate

A will means probate. Probate means lack of privacy, wasted money, and maybe some hard feelings to boot. Avoid probate

There are two kinds of people in the legal world; there is the natural person and the non-natural person.

Legal People | Two Kinds

There are two kinds of people in the legal world; there is the natural person and the non-natural person.

A natural person is a person like you or me, a person who was given life by being born of a human mother. A non-natural person is a person like a trust or corporation, a person who was given life by someone signing a document. Both are legal entities that have legal rights. Both can transact business; both can own, buy, sell, give away, or transfer property.

A Revocable Living Trust (RLT) is a non-natural person, a legal entity; it can own, buy, sell, give away, or transfer property. It can do anything with property you can do.

How can an RLT own, buy, sell, give away, or transfer property? It's simple. Just like a corporation does what its President directs it to do, an RLT does what its Trustee directs it to do. General Motors was directed by its President to make and sell cars; so, it makes and sells cars. Likewise, an RLT does what it's told to do by its Trustee.

How does this physically happen? When the President of General Motors instructs GM to buy some steel to make cars, the President signs the purchase order "on behalf of" General Motors. When he does that, the natural person, the President, is holding the pen when the document is signed; but, the action is legally taking place by the non-natural person, General Motors; so, the steel is being bought by the corporation General Motors.

The President has the power, as President, to sign for, and obligate, the corporation. It works the same way with a Revocable Living Trust. When you want to sell a piece of

The key to making this work is HOW the documents are signed.

property that's in your trust, you, the natural person, simply sign the closing documents "on behalf of" the trust. When you do that, the natural person, the Trustee, is holding the pen when the document is signed; but, the action is legally taking place by the non-natural person, your RLT; so, the property is being sold by your trust. YOU have the power, as Trustee, to sign for, and obligate, the trust.

The key to making this work is HOW the documents are signed. If the President signed something personal for himself, like his driver's license, he would sign it: Bob Smith. But, if he signed something business for General Motors, like the purchase order for steel, he would sign it: Geneal Motors BY Bob Smith, President. It's the same with a Revocable Living Trust. When you want your RLT to do something, you will sign on behalf of your trust: The Havey J. Smith Revocable Trust by Harvey J. Smith, Trustee.

Avoiding probate is easy.

Revocable Trust | No Probate

Avoiding probate is easy. You simply create a Revocable Living Trust by signing a Declaration of Trust document; then, you transfer your assets to your RLT before you die.

With your RLT, you do the same things you would do with your will; you say what you want to be done with your assets when you die. The difference is that assets transferred to your heirs by way of your will are subject to probate; assets transferred to your heirs by your RLT are not.

- Your RLT is private; it is NOT recorded at the courthouse. So, other than your heirs, no one knows what you had or to whom you left it.

- Your RLT is probate expense free. Since it does NOT go through probate, there are no probate fees; that is, no court costs or attorney fees.

- Your RLT is easier on the family. There is NO probate; it's a family-oriented way to handle your affairs.

Make another list of all of your personal property without a title, like the heirloom watch that your klepto great, great, great, great uncle stole from Napoleon.

Getting Started

The first thing to do is list all of your assets. List your house, bank accounts, brokerage accounts, life insurance policies, annuities, IRA accounts, 401k accounts, etc. Make another list of all of your personal property without a title, like the heirloom watch that your klepto great, great, great, great uncle stole from Napoleon.

The next thing to do is list the people to whom you would like to leave something when you die. Be thorough: list each person's full name, address, phone number and email address. If you have their date of birth, list that too. Include as much information as you can to make it easy to find and identify them when the time comes. Remember, it's your money; you can leave it to whomever you want. Don't forget to consider your favorite charity.

The next thing to do is decide who gets what. You can do that by percentages, or by specific item, or by a combination of both. For example, perhaps you want all of your assets to be divided equally between your adult son and adult daughter; or, perhaps you want all of your assets to be divided equally between your adult son and adult daughter, with the ONE exception that you want your Napoleon watch to go to your best friend.

The next thing to decide is how your heirs get their inheritance; do they get it all at once, or in installments over time?For example, let's say you have a minor child, and you don't think it would be a good idea to give him 6 trillion dollars when he's 18 years old. With an RLT, you can direct that the child receives his inheritance in installments, perhaps one at age 18, another at age 25, another at age 30, etc., with distributions between for health, education, and welfare purposes.

Even if your children are young adults, you might want to give them their inheritance over time.

Even if your children are young adults, you might want to give them their inheritance over time. For example, Johnny Jr. might be a fine young man; nonetheless, you might think it a good idea to give him 25% of his inheritance immediately, then 25% five years later, then 25% five years after that, then the balance in another five years. Distributing the inheritance in installments is an especially good idea if you have younger heirs. It gives them a chance to practice handling money with the first distribution, and it gives them a chance to make some mistakes and learn from them. That's code for spending every last penny on a new Ferrari, wine, women, and song.

If you structure the payouts, you might want to allow additional access to the money for reasons of health care, education, and well-being. What good is a trust fund if a person has serious medical needs and can't afford treatment, or wants to get an education but has no money for tuition, or loses his job and is about to lose his house?

Whatever the case might be, with a Revocable Living Trust, you have the post-death capacity to manage your assets from the grave. You cannot do this with just a will.

YOU will run the show because you will be the Trustee.

Who Runs the Show

After you decide who gets what, you need to decide who will handle things.

During your life, YOU will run the show because you will be the Trustee. Almost nothing will change. You will transfer your assets to your trust, and then you will continue to live your life as you did before.

For example, the title on your checking account will change from Harvey J. Smith to The Harvey J. Smith Revocable Trust. Other than the ownership of the checking account, and the name change, everything else will stay the same. You will continue to sign your checks the same way that you always have. I said "almost" nothing will change because there will be one very big difference. If you die before you do this, your checking account titled in your name WILL go through probate; but, if you do this before you die, your checking account titled in the name of your trust WILL NOT go through probate. It's the same with the rest of your assets. As soon as you transfer them to your trust, they're out of the reach of probate. THIS is a BIG issue. You would not believe how many people I've met during my practice who established a Revocable Living Trust and then failed to transfer their assets to it. They WASTED their time and money in setting up their trust: an "unfunded" RLT is useless.

After your death, your "Successor Trustee" will run the show. This is the person who manages your trust in your absence. Your absence might be because of your death, or it might be because of your incompetency. Therein lies the wisdom in naming a "Medical Committee" in your RLT, a group of people who KNOW you. If they see you suddenly standing on the street corner handing out $100.00 bills, they will KNOW whether or not standing on

There are two kinds of Trustees and Successor Trustees.

the street corner handing out $100.00 bills is something that you would do. If it isn't, they can step in and take over, and get you some help. Your Medical Committee can be family, friends or strangers, or a combination, and it can be changed at any time by executing a simple amendment. It's interesting how relationships change with time; someone who might be a good Medical Committee candidate today might not be tomorrow.

There are two kinds of Trustees and Successor Trustees. There are natural person Trustees, like you or me; and there are non-natural person Trustees, like a bank. Regardless of which kind of Successor Trustee you choose, natural or non-natural, the responsibilities are the same.

Your Successor Trustee is bound by the terms of the trust to handle the trust assets as you have instructed. He has a FIDUCIARY RESPONSIBILITY to you and to the heirs of your trust. Under the law, a fiduciary responsibility is the highest responsibility that a person can have. A person who holds a fiduciary responsibility must follow the PRUDENT MAN RULE; that is, he must handle the affairs of the person for whom he holds a fiduciary responsibility "as would a prudent man handle his own affairs."

Use careful consideration when picking a Successor Trustee; not everyone qualifies under these strict guidelines. Pick someone to serve as your Successor Trustee who is intelligent and honest. Pick someone who genuinely cares about you and your heirs, someone who will do what's right for your heirs, someone who will put their interests first. This is the kind of person you should look for to serve as your Successor Trustee.

The strength of picking a natural person to serve as yourSuccessor Trustee is the personal touch he or she

The strength of picking a natural person to serve as your Successor Trustee is the personal touch he or she will bring to the effort: "someone who genuinely cares about you and your heirs."

will bring to the effort: "someone who genuinely cares about you and your heirs." That person knows your heirs and can make decisions on their behalf that make sense for them.

The weaknesses of picking a natural person to serve as your Successor Trustee are human mortality and human frailty. No one knows when he or she will die, and even the best of us can change, for the worse, if sufficiently motivated. Think of the best person you know. If his family was kidnapped, and he was ordered to steal the money from your trust to pay a ransom or his family would be murdered, what would he do? What would you do if you were in his position? You take my point.

The strength of picking a non-natural person, such as your bank, to serve as your Successor Trustee is the corporate guarantee. If you name a bank to serve as your Successor Trustee, and the banker in charge of handling your trust steals the money from your trust, the bank must make good on the loss. That's the strength of picking a non-natural person to serve as your Successor Trustee: the corporate guarantee.

The weakness of picking a non-natural person to serve as your Successor Trustee is the lack of personal knowledge about your heirs. The banker assigned to handle your trust doesn't know your heirs, so how can he be expected to make judgement calls on behalf of a person he doesn't know? Most bankers whom I've met have been good people who try to do a good job, but good intentions can only get you so far. When something comes up that requires a judgement call from the non-natural Successor Trustee, and it will come up, the non-natural just can't make the call and your heirs will lose by default.

Pick a natural person and take a chance on your heirs getting robbed, or pick a non-natural person and leave your heirs at the mercy of an impersonal corporation?

So, what to do? Pick a natural person and take a chance on your heirs getting robbed, or pick a non-natural person and leave your heirs at the mercy of an impersonal corporation? I suggest, NEITHER; pick BOTH to serve as Successor CO-Trustees.

Pick someone who is intelligent and honest; someone who genuinely cares about you and your heirs; a person who knows you and your heirs well enough to make personal judgment calls on your behalf. Then, pick a bank to serve as Successor "Co-Trustee." That's the best of both worlds. Neither can write a check unless both sign off, and even if one did for untoward purposes, the corporate guarantee would be in place.

What if the Successor Co-Trustees don't agree, or just can't seem to work together? You name a bank to serve as Successor Co-Trustee, and you give your natural person Successor Co-Trustee the power to replace. If he doesn't like working with the banker from the first bank, he has the right to fire the bank and replace it with another bank. If he can't get along with the second, he has the right to replace it with the third, and so on, indefinitely.Often there's more to the issue of the "power to replace" than your Successor Trustee just not liking to work with the banker in charge; there is the issue of fees. Banks charge fees for serving as Trustee or Co-Trustee, and sometimes even the minimum fees can be pretty stiff, especially for a smaller account. By giving your Successor Trustee the power to replace, you give him the opportunity to negotiate the fees.

I once received a call from a woman whom I had known in high school. I had been hot for her in school because she was hot (still is), but after a couple of dates she wouldn't give me the time of day (still won't). She told her mother, who told her brother, who told everyone on Planet Earth

Not one penny had been earned to benefit the daughter in 10 years. That's how expensive bank fees can be. It was all perfectly legal.

I "just didn't turn her on." But I digress, back to the matter at hand. She told me that her minor daughter had been injured in an accident, had received a settlement, and that the courts had named a bank to serve as trustee. She said that it had been 10 years since the settlement money had been deposited, there had been no withdrawals from the account, and there was still exactly the same amount of money in the account as had been deposited 10 years before. She asked me to review the trust documents, so I did. As it turned out, the interest that the account had earned had been used up in bank fees and attorney fees. The bank's attorney had been called in every year to "review the documents." Not one penny had been earned to benefit the daughter in 10 years. That's how expensive bank fees can be. It was all perfectly legal.

I once received a call from a retired old woman who had a mentally challenged son; he was in his late twenties physically, but about 15 mentally. In consideration of her advanced age, the old woman had put her son's inheritance in a trust at the bank. The conditions of the trust provided for his "health, education, and welfare." When she contacted the banker handling the trust to make a withdrawal so she could help her son pay for his car insurance and license plates, the banker refused. He said the expenses didn't qualify under the "health, education, and welfare" clause. That's how cold and impersonal a corporate trustee can be. The poor woman asked me if there was anything that I could do, so I had a little chat with the banker about the lawsuit that might be filed asking the court to replace his bank with another as Trustee; he dispersed the funds.

I told the woman to call me if she had any more problems. She called me about six months later to tell me she didn't understand it, but Mr. Smith at the bank had become one of the nicest people she had ever met. Praise God for Mr.

That's how cold and impersonal
a corporate trustee can be.

Smith's new attitude, and for the legal right to petition the court to have a Trustee removed.

Now that we're talking about back up non-natural person Successor Co-Trustees, name at least two NATURAL person Successor Co-Trustees in the order in which you prefer them to serve. At the time of your death, the first one might not be willing or able to serve, so the second on the list might have to be called up to active duty.

Might not be "willing" to serve? That's right. Things change. Your best friend or adult child might be willing and able to serve as your Successor Co-Trustee on the day you ask him, but by the time the need arises his life might have changed so drastically that it just isn't possible for him to serve. So, you name more than one, in the order of your preference. Technically, they're called your First Successor Co-Trustee, and you Second Successor Co-Trustee.

This brings up a good point about asking your friend if he will serve as your Successor Co-Trustee. Doing so does no good, because he doesn't know until the time comes what he will want to do or be able to do and asking him just puts him on the spot. If he is your friend, he will take the request very seriously, and he might feel compelled to decline if he feels he might not be able to serve. That can be awkward; why put a friend in this position? I suggest you name the people whom you want to serve, but you don't mention it to them; let them decide if and when the time comes. The same thing holds for the banks you name; just make sure the banks you name have a trust department.

Once you have made these decisions and collected the information, you're almost ready to meet with your

Might not be “willing” to serve?

attorney to have the documents drafted. First, you need to consider some other documents.

A will? Why would I need to think about a will?

Other Documents

There are several other documents you need to consider before you meet with your attorney to have your Revocable Living Trust drafted.

Will

There are two kinds of wills; a regular will, sometimes called a testamentary will, that is used when a person doesn't have a Revocable Living Trust, and a Pour-Over Will used in tandem with an RLT. The words "pour-over" are the key. The Pour-Over Will states that if any assets were not transferred to your RLT, they will be immediately transferred, they will "pour over" into your trust.

You might be thinking, "A will? Why would I need to think about a will? I thought I didn't need a will, because I'm going to transfer my assets to my heirs by way of my RLT." If you're thinking that, you're right, partly. You ARE going to transfer your assets to your heirs by way of your RLT and thereby avoid probate; but there are a few things that a will can do that an RLT can't.

For example, if you have minor children, you will dictate in your RLT how you want their assets handled, but you will nominate in your will whom you want to raise your children until they are of age. I say NOMINATE because the judge will make the final decision; usually the wishes of the deceased parents are considered heavily, and normally followed.

For the same reason that you don't ask your friend if he will be your Successor Trustee, you shouldn't ask your friend if he will raise your children if you die. Just nominate him in your will and let him decide at the time of death. Nominate two or three, in the order of preference. "I nominate my brother John H. Smith to raise my children until they are

...you shouldn't ask your friend if he will raise your children if you die.

of legal age, unless he is unable or unwilling to serve, in which case I name my uncle Dr. Hannibal Lecter..."

Another example is a wrongful death lawsuit. If you are killed in an accident, and there is sufficient reason to believe that another person's negligence is to blame, your estate may file a wrongful death suit. Then, if your estate wins a settlement, your Pour-Over Will, will transfer the settlement to your RLT so the proceeds can be handled in accordance with your other assets. So, you will need a Pour-Over Will to go with your Revocable Living Trust.

One more thing about wills. Even if you think you don't have a will, you DO have a will, you just don't know it. Every state has on the books its Laws of Intestacy. These laws dictate how a person's estate will be handled if they die without having gone to the trouble of having a will drafted. These laws act as your will, so to speak. So, the question is, do you want to decide what will happen to your assets, and do you at least want a chance to nominate who will raise your minor children; or do you want to just let some strange probate judge do it? It's your call. No one really cares except maybe you care, and maybe your heirs care, and maybe your orphaned children care.

Living Will | Life Prolonging Procedures Declaration

A Living Will declares that if you are brain dead you do not want your body to be kept alive by artificial means. A Life Prolonging Procedures Declaration declares the opposite. As an act of compassion for your heirs, you should make the decision as to what you want to happen and have the appropriate document drafted.

Memorandum of Trust

A Memorandum of Trust attests that you DO have a

A Living Will declares that if you are brain dead
you do not want your body to be kept
alive by artificial means.

Revocable Living Trust, that you ARE the Trustee of your trust, and that you DO have all the powers associated thereto. This is a very important document, especially when transferring assets to your trust, or changing beneficiaries on life insurance policies or annuities so that the proceeds are payable to your trust. Without the Memorandum of Trust, you may be compelled to produce the entire RLT and thereby relinquish its privacy. You don't have to do anything, or make any decisions, to have a Declaration of Trust other than making sure your attorney prepares one when he drafts your trust; some attorneys do it automatically, others don't.

Revocable Assignment Agreement

A Revocable Assignment Agreement transfers all of your untitled assets to your trust. You have only to sign it, and the tee shirt you are wearing is no longer part of your probate estate, it's in your RLT. The same goes for your expensive jewelry, works of art, and Napoleon watch. You might be surprised how quickly the value of untitled personal property can add up. A Revocable Assignment Agreement can save your heirs a lot of money. It's REVOCABLE, meaning the assets that it transfers to your trust do not have to stay in your trust. You can sell the tee shirt and use the money to buy another any time you wish.

Power of Attorney

There are two kinds of Power of Attorney. A General Durable Power of Attorney gives the person to whom you give power TOTAL AND ABSOLUTE power to do whatever they feel should be done. A Limited Power of Attorney gives the person to whom you give power LIMITED POWER to do only that which you specify. You should have at least a Limited Power of Attorney drafted that gives your Successor Trustee (or anyone else you

A Revocable Assignment Agreement can
save your heirs a lot of money.

choose) the power to transfer assets to your trust. That's it, that all your Limited Power of Attorney will do; it will empower your Successor Trustee to transfer any assets that you might have that were not transferred to your trust.

You may ask why this document is necessary because you are planning to transfer all of your assets to your trust; and you would be asking a logical question. There might be a time when you receive an asset, and you cannot transfer it to your trust. You aren't non compos mentis (mentally incompetent), so your Medical Committee can't step in and help, but you cannot transfer the asset. That's when the Limited Power of Attorney is useful; it gives your Successor Trustee the power to do what needs to be done.

Appointment of Health Care Representative

An Appointment of Health Care Representative is a document you use to appoint someone to make medical decisions for you if you cannot make them for yourself.

There was once a race car driver in a coma after an accident. The doctors wanted to remove his right arm. His mother was his health care representative, and she knew that he would NOT want his right arm removed, regardless of the reasons. So, she refused to let the doctors remove her son's right arm. When the son came to, he spoke with the doctors about why they wanted to remove his arm. Then he decided to keep his right arm. As time went by, he regained some use of it.

The moral of the story is, choose someone to be your health care representative who knows you, and who has a pretty good idea as to what you would want done if you were able to communicate your wishes.

There was once a race car driver in a coma
after an accident.

I once called my mother and told her that while I didn't like talking about her death, some things needed to be done beforehand, one of which was the creation of a document naming a health care representative. I explained the concept to her, and I explained some of the other documents that needed to be drafted. I explained to her it would cost her nothing to get this work done, that I would handle it. She listened politely, and then she said that she would talk to Jeffrey about it and let me know. Jeffrey is my baby brother; I'm the oldest of five boys, he's the youngest. Jeffrey has a degree in safety management; as far as anyone knows, he has no formal training in estate planning. But, since he DID serve as an EMT when he was on the volunteer fire department, Mother has considered him to be the family doctor whom we should all consult when a medical need arises.

Apparently, the wisdom one gains from being an EMT extends beyond being a doctor to being an expert in estate planning as well. Who knew? Mother called me the next day and said that Jeffrey didn't think it would be necessary to draft a document naming a health care representative. It wasn't a matter of money; he just didn't think that it was necessary. So, Mother followed Doctor/Attorney Jeffrey's advice and declined my offer to help.

Two weeks later, Mother had a medical problem and went into a coma. The Brothers Four called in a panic and asked what they should do. I told them they needed to hire an attorney and petition the court to have a temporary guardian appointed to make decisions on Mother's behalf. They said okay. The next day they called and wanted to know if I would help with the legal fees.

Fortunately, Mother made a full and complete recovery. After she was back at home, I suggested to her we

Apparently, the wisdom one gains from being an EMT extends beyond being a doctor to being an expert in estate planning as well. Who knew?

revisit the idea of some estate planning; specifically, the appointment of a health care representative. She listened politely, and said that she would talk to Jeffrey...

The moral of the story? Every family has its Jeffrey. Get your legal advice from a LAWYER.

Do NOT try to draft your own documents; do NOT try to modify your uncle Bob's documents to fit your need; do NOT buy a will and trust kit off the internet and do it yourself for $14.95.

See the Attorney

NOW it's time to see the attorney and have your documents drafted. Do NOT try to draft your own documents; do NOT try to modify your uncle Bob's documents to fit your need; do NOT buy a will and trust kit off the internet and do it yourself for $14.95. Find a good lawyer, one WHO WENT TO LAW SCHOOL TO LEARN HOW TO DO WILLS AND TRUSTS and hire him to do your wills and trusts. Would you try to do your own heart surgery? This is just as important, and the consequences of a botched job are just as dire, almost.

How do you find a good lawyer to draft your wills and trusts? That's simple, at least in concept. Find an attorney who does estate planning; he'll know more about it than one who specializes in wrongful death suits. Then, ask him what set of documents he thinks you might need, and see if he mentions the documents that I've discussed herein. If the attorney you are considering specializes in estate planning, and he understands the documents discussed herein, there's a good chance he will do a good job for you. Suggestion: do some price shopping for fees. Your goal is to transfer your assets to your heirs for their enjoyment, not to the attorney who drafted your documents.

Speaking of lawyers, don't believe everything that you hear about them. I've been in this game a long time, and the vast majority of the lawyers that I've met have been high-caliber people who work hard to do a good job for their clients. Of course there are the ones who don't try so hard, the ones whose performance is disappointing (I know, I've hired a few), but they are the exceptions, they are the small minority.

After you have your documents done, and your assets transferred, it's a good idea to have a family meeting

After you have your documents done, and your assets transferred, it's a good idea to have a family meeting and review them.

and review them. Doing so will give your heirs a sense of well-being, a sense of equilibrium. It will also be a good opportunity to train your children on how things should be done. It will help expand their world view and give them a better sense of how to operate. I recommend an annual review. Even if things haven't changed much, an annual family estate planning review is a strong idea.

Will and trust planing isn't just about money.

I'm Smith, Not Gates!

I don't like to use the words "estate planning" when I'm talking to an everyday, normal American, because the very words conjure up mental images of great wealth. That leads the everyday American to think that he or she doesn't need to do any estate planning, that is, will and trust planning. In reality, nothing could be further from the truth.

Will and trust planning isn't just about money; it's about having what you DO have handled how you want it to be handled, and it's about treating the people you leave behind with compassion and respect by showing them you care enough about their well-being to do some planning. Quality estate planning is a low-key way of saying "I love you, and I care about you." It's a very high-caliber thing to do.

Index

Public Notice

The author is not an attorney, nor does he give legal advice. The reader is advised to seek legal counsel regarding his estate planning, including, but not limited to, the concepts discussed. Neither the publisher nor the author accepts any liability for any consequences resulting from reading this book.

Jim Clark is an award-winning internationally-published author. He is the recipient of the International Poetry Society's coveted Editor's Choice Award for his outstanding book of romantic poems:

May I Dream?

A collection of poems on matters of the heart.

Jim Clark Books

Jim Clark books are exciting. There are four genres: Retirement Planning, Romance, Life on Earth, and Textbooks. Regardless of whether you're feeling romantic, planning your retirement, protecting your estate, or preparing for a new career, you'll find the right book in Jim Clark's outstanding collection.

Jim Clark books carry a three-fold purpose: to inform, to entertain, and to raise awareness that there are children in America who go to bed hungry. Profits from Jim Clark's books are donated to feeding hungry American children.

Jim Clark books are J. Charles Clark Publishing publications. This and other outstanding books by the author may be purchased at:

www.jimclarkbooks.com

To learn how you can help feed every hungry child in America visit

jimclarkamerican.com/children.

Made in the USA
Monee, IL
04 November 2026

67385490R10036